Things Found after the Fire

Things Found after the Fire

Written by Sean Voisin
(Also Signed SV)

Edited by Rita Magallona

ISBN-13: 978-0692916001(GoodVibes Publishers)
ISBN-10: 0692916008

Dedication

I wrote this for us, dear reader.

We are but wandering souls.

Our journeys may have already been decided,

but still, we push through the fire.

That's when we'll discover what we are capable of.

We'll find things we didn't dare to imagine.

After the fire, I found love, heartbreak, and inspiration.

Walks along the Trail

My whole life thus far, I have stumbled,

been bruised, fell, and got

back up again.

I have quietly felt the weight of the world on my shoulders.

I stumbled when my dad died two weeks before my graduation.

I stumbled when that relationship I wanted to work didn't go as planned.

Through pain, through tears, through anguish, through love—

through it all,

We learn who we are and

who we are becoming; like a phoenix, despite it all

we still rise.

Contents

Chapter One: Love

Chapter Two: Heartbreak

Chapter Three: Healing/Inspiration

Chapter One: Love

The Eyes Can Tell

Please understand that love shouldn't hurt you.
It doesn't mentally abuse you; it doesn't assault you.
Loving hands are gentle to the touch.
His shame will not define you.
Your strength to leave will sustain you.
You're beautiful; your strength will heal you.
Baby girl, please understand we need you.

Rolling Stone

She was like a baby taking her first step, legs wobbling as she placed one foot in front of the other.
Before she knew it, she was running.
This is exactly how she fell in love, but no one ever told her about the fall.
That the fall would hurt every time she fell.
Some falls hurt more than others. But still, she let it go. Like a baby, she kept taking her first step until she met him—someone who was able to catch her almost every time.

Please Understand

You're not too loud; you're not too quiet.
You're not too fat; you're not too skinny.
You're not too tall; you're not too short.
You're not too outgoing; you're not too shy.
You're not too much to handle.
The things they are complaining about are the very same things someone else is searching for.
Someone out there is searching for someone just like you.
So if they don't appreciate you,
don't worry;
The right person will find you.

Happiness

I found love when I stopped looking for it.
I found joy when I offered kindness.
I found favor when I started forgiving.
I found happiness when I focused on the positive.

Rewards

Love takes sacrifice.
It takes strength.
It takes courage.
It takes honesty.
Too often, we believe rewards should be given
without all of the above.

Unplanned Steps

So much of life is unplanned.
I never expected to fall in love, but I did.
I planned for a vacation, but the weather changed.
I planned for a trip, believing foresight was at my
fingertips.
But the stops in my destination made me realize
that something else controlled these steps of mine.

Walking

Sometimes, you're forced to lift,
and when you do it, you discover how strong you are.
How fiercely capable you are of dealing with the cards
you've been dealt.
So just be as you are, and see it through.
Just breathe.

A Secret Ingredient

Happiness is like a secret ingredient.
Sometimes, the magic
is in the hands that prepare it.

A Perfect Fit

She was a perfect fit. Once she understood that, it was easy for her to let go all of the people who didn't appreciate her worth.

My Best Friend

My mom was my best friend
long before I even understood what a best friend was.
She has been with me
through the tough parts of my life and the best of
times.

Committed Relationships

Committed relationships are just like plants.
If they are not watered,
they will surely die.

Compass

Love can be like the wind.
You cannot see it,
but you can surely feel it.
It shapes the people around us
just like how the wind determines
which way the tree blows.

Distance

Don't let the fear of being alone keep you from getting what you really deserve.

Beauty in a Harsh World

She grew in the harsh confines of this world,
curving and weaving her way to sunlight,
eventually blossoming into what she was meant to be:
a beautiful rose, inside and out.

Music

Sometimes it takes the right angle, and I'm a math
major, kind of like the right timing—
beautiful.
I just want you to stand by my side as we take trips
together, pics together.
I just want to admire us.
I'll spin you in circles; I'll drive you wild sometimes,
but I'll always be gentle.
At the end of the day, no one wants to dance forever,
all alone.

Yes

One day, I'm going to ask you a question—
a question that many women often dream of.
And you're going to give me the short answer.

But you see, you've been saying yes the entire time
we've been dating.
When I asked you to visit me in Brazil
and you drove four hours to JFK Airport
just to spend an extra day with me,
You said yes then.

When you took the time to listen about my situation at
work and helped me see things from a different
perceptive,
You said yes then.

When all you needed was my company to have a good
time,
You said yes then.

When you took the time to understand me for who I
am,
You said yes then.

You see, I realize it's not about the fairy-tale ending or
that short answer
but the times that lead up to it
and the battles we overcome.

That Spark

A woman can immediately feel if a spark is there or if it isn't.

Uncertainty

She is stuck in between happiness and contentment
at the beginning of good but not at the end of great.
Her heart doesn't flicker as it should,
but her mind doesn't overthink as it would.
Her excitement and butterflies aren't there,
but she doesn't have to worry about Cupid not playing
fair.

Maybe her mind could convince her heart that it
should,
and maybe it would,
because loving someone and being in love with
someone
can change the weight of your world.

Addicted

She got so accustomed to being hurt
that it became normal to her.
By the time she met someone
who actually showed her love,
it was too late
because by then,
she was already addicted to the pain.

Moments along the Trail

Everything in life has moments:
moments to love,
moments to cry,
moments to smile,
moments to laugh,
moments to enjoy every waking morning where the
sunlight dances around your skin, and moments to
remember that even after the bad times, there will still
be more good moments.

You Can Breathe

Don't worry;
I'm going to treat you with gentle hands,
because I can tell
the world has been so tough on you.

Imagine

Imagine if we could get a cup of love
just like we get a cup of coffee or tea.
Imagine just drinking it and thinking,
"Hmm, I needed that this morning."

Fruit

We live in a world that places so much value on image and appeal. So much glitter that we almost forget to look for gold.

Moonlight

You are a blessing. Someone out there is looking for someone just like you.

A Sad Dance

We took so many steps
back and forth from each other
emotionally
without ever moving our feet.

Destination

Even when we had different views,
when we were at different places in life,
All those things made no difference
because our destination was the same;
That destiny led me to you.

Shadows

I saw your shadow in the morning,
and just the thought of you being there
made everything all right.

Warmth

Love will find you in the simplest of ways. That, I promise.

Time Spent Away

So much time spent on the train,
so much time spent traveling,
but everything that took me further away from you
was the very same things that brought me back.
The more I traveled,
the more I realized there's none quite like you, and
there isn't any quite like us.

Simple Can Work Sometimes

There's simplicity in her that's timeless like a river.

There's simplicity in her beauty.
It isn't forced.
Something from within her shines out,
illuminating her skin in a way that no cosmetic can
ever mimic.

There's simplicity in her values.
They remind me of a fresh summer morning,
like the ones from the days of old.

Walking along the Beach

Love—such a simple and complicated thing.
Everyone knows it, but not everyone understands it all
the time.
Love—the thing that can tear you apart swiftly
and put you back together at the same time.

Friends

I first called you my friend, not because I didn't find you special
but because of how special I found you.
You see, girlfriends come and go,
but there's a friend who will last a lifetime.
Sometimes, the heart is more forgiving to a friend than to a boyfriend.
Sometimes, the heart just needs a friend.

Ultimately, you're so much more than a friend.
The word "friend" clearly doesn't define how special you are to me.
But if friends can last a lifetime, then maybe a friend isn't such a bad thing,
because the thought of me losing you
makes me uncomfortable.

Rising Tide

There's a passion that grows inside you,
like the ocean that's affected by the moon.
You feel your instincts kicking in,
and your steady waters are no longer still.
Sometimes, you have to follow that rising tide.

World

They say you can see the world in someone's eyes, and, at first, I doubted it. But when I gazed into your eyes, I realized exactly what they meant.

Stand Tall, Soldier

She was always Daddy's little girl.
The last time she saw him was in a picture—
a picture of him dressed in a uniform before he left.

A Blind Fall

They say love is blind.
My friends pointed out the obvious,
And at first, so did I.
But like hail in the summertime,
sometimes you're hit hard by the unexpected.
Maybe that's why they say you're falling
instead of walking in love
Because whoever expects to fall?

It's All in the Eyes

With only her eyes
and a simple smile,
she showed me her vulnerability.

The Strength of a Woman

It was her strength that made me like her,
and it was her vulnerability that made me love her—
the brittle tenderness of a woman's embrace.

Diamonds

Sometimes, it takes a gift,
a special set of eyes, to appreciate a diamond.
So understand you're not going to be for everyone,
and that's okay.

Happiness

What is happiness but a selection of memories?
Where the hope of them occurring again is stronger
than the doubt.

Hostage

At that moment, she realized that she was done—
done waiting for someone who was mentally and
emotionally gone.
No longer would she remain hostage by past
memories.

Attraction

She was attracted by intelligence.
It was a beauty that seduced her mind.

I Miss You Sometimes

Sometimes you miss someone, and it's okay. It just means you're human, but the reality is you don't have to go back to that person; it's okay to move on.

Your Mind and Heart

Your heart is usually where your mind resides. Who are you thinking of, and why?

It's Not Always Pretty

Sometimes, for things to work,
it doesn't all have to make sense.
Sometimes, there's beauty in the unorganized.
Sometimes, love is messy.

Hi, There

Sometimes, someone comes into your life,
reminding you how special you are, reminding you
that every bad relationship that took place was just a
stepping-stone.

In Hot Pursuit

Smiles, curiosity, good conversations—she is in pursuit of what happens next.

Wisdom

Sometimes it takes strength to leave; it takes strength to walk away from that toxic relationship.

Written for You

I wrote this just for you—
to let you know, have no fear.
Put all your worries aside.
I wrote this just for you—
to let you know that I care.

Not for Sharing

Please protect our connection.
Don't share it with your friends.
I don't want signals to get crossed.

Please protect our connection.
If I say something wrong, let me know.
If I mess up, forgive me.
I'll learn.

Just please protect our connection.
Don't share it with friends.
It's a busy world around us.
No need to share our Wi-Fi code.

Stupid in Love

Doesn't love call out to you?
Can't you hear it?
You follow it to the person whom you think it's
coming from,
like a rabbit running through a maze,
only to be disappointed
when you run into a dead end.
But love still calls, and you still follow.

Dimples

I found the silver lining
in the dimples of her smile.

No, Wait

A man who loves you
will see past your beauty and understand that it is only
part of who you are.
He will see past your flaws and fall in love with your
soul.
So even when you have a bad day and you eventually
age, to him
you will always be beautiful.

Hourglass

She was like the last
grain of sand to hit
the hourglass.
Imperfect.
But
to me,
she was all
the woman I needed.

Secrets

Your scars will never tell lies.
The wrinkles by your eyes
show me a woman who wasn't afraid to smile.
The stretch marks over your body
let me know your curves are real.
And your eyes,
your eyes let me know you just want to be loved.

Honest Love

Find someone who wants to get to know you for you, not just your appearance; getting to know you is like finding hidden treasures. Find you a captain who's ready for that treasure hunt.

What Does It Take?

The truth is love takes time.
It is forgiving.
It is patient.

The truth is the type of love you are looking for
takes time in getting to know that person—
the good, the bad, the ugly, and the reality.

The truth is love can take time.
It is not measured by time,
but it takes time.

Your Heart Decides?

No one can tell your heart whom to love—
not your parents, not your friends, no one.
But at the end of the day,
know your worth.

What Do You Really Want?

She desired to be loved. Ultimately, that's what she really wanted.

Staying the Course

There's always going to be more than one reason to
say no.
But the right person for you will always find a way to
make it work.
You never really have to ask for love;
love finds a way.

Grasping Reality

Some people say the person who holds onto the relationship the longest gets hurt the most. The truth is you hold onto God first, and then everything else falls in line.

I Know You

Before expecting someone to love you, you must first understand how to love yourself. So when love comes along, you recognize it.

Worth More than Gold

Love has no monetary value. People who often seek love through monetary gain often find themselves shortchanged.

Value

The love money can't buy is the most expensive love
of them all.

Dining In

Sometimes a woman just wants to spend time with you, time in the house, sharing laughs; sometimes simplicity is best.

Chapter Two: Heartbreak

My Very First

My first love was like my first real bicycle experience.
The joy I felt riding with no training wheels:
the wind,
the excitement,
the freedom.

But the fall,
I didn't see that coming.
It hurt like hell.
But I'm glad I never forgot how to ride my bike.
But I did learn how to brace for a fall.

Truth

If I give you the truth, it's worth its value in gold.
But the weight of it will weigh heavily on your soul,
breaking your perception of reality.
So should I share the truth
or spare you a lie?

Death

You are gone, but in my dreams I always find you. I find you in a still place, where the joy of seeing you again takes away any sorrow that I ever felt when I lost you. So in my dreams, I will always find you.

Forgetting

When a loved one passes away, you often never forget the last time you saw that person; the last time stays with you forever. Like a light that stays dim on your mind, reminding you of a memory that seems to last a lifetime. A memory that reminds you of a time line that strings together your past and future; the truth is I miss you all the time.

Grudges

Love hurts sometimes, and that's okay—don't let the pain overtake you; forgive and move on.

The Importance of Setbacks

Baby, look: after all these setbacks, you still rise, and you will not stop going.

Exposed

The world can be like a small beach. All things done in secret will soon come to shore.

Baggage

The more you hold onto hurt, the more bags you have to carry. Eventually all those bags will weigh you down.

Learning the Hard Way

Placing your hand on a hot stove
after you've just been burned:
that's what it is like
when you don't learn from your mistakes.

Lost Dreams

Like a snowflake that falls to the ground before its
intended time,
drying up without leaving its intended mark—
that is the same as a dream deferred.

It's Not Real

He tries to impress you with glitter, but you are not impressed by his mind. You have seen many like him, and this time you will not fall for it.

Fifteen Minutes of Fame

He likes you, and you get it, but your heart yearns for
something more, something money can't ever buy,
deeper than just flowers. So you move on, in search of
a love that's real to the core.

Bad Memories

These streetlights shall flicker forever.
I am stuck with the constant reminder of what
occurred or what I did.
A history of time trapped in my mind that's on a
perpetual loop,
reminding me of a tragedy that's commonly not
spoken of
but haunts the deepest parts of my soul.

Reflections

The heart of a person is affected by ripple effects, just like the water that crashes upon the sand.
A mother is torn because her husband died.
A son is scorned because his father isn't around.
A daughter mourns because she's in search of a father figure.

Emotions crash from one figure to another.
A boyfriend is hurt because his love isn't reciprocated.
His perception of love is ultimately defined from his first impression of love. Emotions translate from one person to another, changing their minds based on past reflections.

Now, the two who were supposed to meet crash upon one another due to past experiences.
She is afraid to love because she was cheated on.
He is impatient because his time was wasted.
Both waves come crashing upon the sands of time, and their ideal moment is gone forever.

Glass

Sometimes, I wish I were like glass.
So the times I do not want to be seen, people can see right past me.
Sometimes, I wish I were like glass so the people I care about can see right through me, into the real me.
Sometimes, I wish I were like glass so I can curve and contour to the situations around me.
Sometimes, I wish I were like glass so I can become bulletproof to those who want to harm me.
Sometimes, I wish I were like glass so that people I dislike will walk right into me.
Sometimes, I wish I were like glass so I can bend and be soft to those who love me.
Sometimes, I wish.

Meaningless

Baby, the mouth cannot convince the heart if the heart is not ready. The heart that loves you will never ever need to be convinced.

Race Tunes

A man who loves you will race to the ocean and back with only your interest keeping him afloat. A woman should never have to chase a man who loves her.

The Depths of a Smile

Sometimes, the saddest heart has the brightest smile.

The Heart Knows

Sometimes, your heart already has the answer.

An Agreement

You should be loved, every part of you, even during your bad hair days.

A Paradox

Funny how the very same person who can make you
so happy
can also be the very same person who can hurt you so
badly.

I Wish

Today was just like any other day.

The alarm went off, the dog barked, and our son played music loud enough for the both of us. I kissed you good-bye and went to work.

At work, on the TV, I saw a plane collide with the World Trade Center. I asked, "What's that movie?"

I found out it was real life taking place.

I sat there, frozen with the weight of the world on my shoulders. My mind was racing, yet I was at a loss for words.

Today was just like any other day.

Except you never came home.

Not Seeing Eye to Eye

The only thing she ever wanted was to know that he cared.

That's It—She Has Had It

He told her: this time was the last time,
and he meant it.
She told him: the last time was the last time,
and she meant it.
When a woman is fed up,
there isn't much a man can do to change her mind.
Pray she doesn't get to that point.

Ignoring Love

She cared so much that she ignored the fact that she did. Because if she accepted the reality of it, it would have made the thought of him even more of a burden to carry.

Chasing Clouds

His head is in the clouds but his face sunken from the trials of his journey. His friends are in dismay. Some family members are in denial, while some try to help. Many are stunned by the extent to which he has become intoxicated by the addiction. Many say his life has no purpose. For him, his purpose is the chase of that elusive high.

Days Dripped By

Days dripped by as if they were minutes, seconds.
I found myself grasping at reality as if it were water in
the palms of my hands. Some feelings
can't be explained; sometimes people fall out of love,
but the fall still hurts.
I've been trying to find my way back home as if I were
a man lost at sea, ever since we broke up.
I guess we needed to let each other go. It still hurts,
but we needed to breathe again, we needed to feel
again.
Sometimes there's beauty in finding the renewed
you—the beauty sometimes comes after the ashes.

Revelation

Time often reveals what was already there.
It's like the unraveling of the truth, slowly revealing
what feelings were buried.
False pretenses were made.
In the end, the only thing left is the naked facts.

From Friends to Strangers

I met you as a stranger.
It's a shame we left each other as such.
From friends
to lovers
to acquaintances.
Now, we no longer talk.
Funny thing is I never expected friends, so why should
I expect a soul mate? I guess sometimes it's the
unexpected that makes us expect the most.

Words Are Needed Too

All she ever wanted was to hear the words; all I ever wanted to do was to show her, so we deferred. Words can be easily said; things can be easily brought, but actions are always going to reveal if someone really cares.

Pride

It was my pride that made me go after her.
She was beautiful, intelligent, and kind.
It was my pride that made me not take no for an
answer.
It was my pride that swept her off her feet.
It was also my pride that made me lose her.
The very same thing that drove me to her was the very
same thing that drove me away.
Pride.

The Anniversary

I think intuition is fascinating. We already know what we want. We often know what we deserve. But yet we ignore the feeling, only to confirm what we already knew years later. Why settle again?

She Made Up Her Mind

Like the season changing, she realized she was no longer going to wait for him. She didn't plan on it; it was simply what she felt. After years of waiting and trying to figure the *it* out, she had reached that point of no return. She had nothing left to give. She had given it her all. I guess when a woman is fed up, there's nothing more she can give.

Crystal Clear

She couldn't remember the last time she cried.
She saw tears run down her left cheek.
But it wasn't intentional; whoever intends to cry?
Maybe her soul knew what her eyes haven't seen yet.
Intuition.

I Lost One

She was my raindrop—unique in her own way.
And although there were many like her, there was
none quite like her.
And when I lost her, it was my tear to shed.
Because a good woman is hard to find

You're Here, and I Still Miss You

Even when you're right in front of me,
it's the thought of you that I miss—
before we both changed,
before the world diluted us.

Freedom

We all want freedom
But when the media stopped telling us what to do,
we stumbled,
as if their chains were training wheels.
Too much TV can spoil a good mind.

Signs

I ignored the signs she gave me. Eventually, I ran the stop sign. I guess someone was bound to get hurt. Who knew that it would be the both of us?

Too Many Saturday Nights

I found happiness at the bottom of the bottle, right next to the cigar tray filled with ashes.

The Depth of Your Heart

Don't be mad if he doesn't understand you. Not everyone can swim in deep waters.

Friends Spoiling Friends

Everyone knows about love and how to make it work.
Friends give each other advice with hopes of making
things right.
Things play out in plain sight.
What may have been spoken in private may have been
all right.

But now with added emotions, the two involved
started to fight
because she was influenced by her friends, and he was
influenced by his.
So many hands were involved in their relationship,
that it ruined their spice.

Where Did They Go?

When I looked up from working, half the people I knew were gone, killed off by my success.

Weather the Storm

Sometimes the storm comes, and you just have to weather it.

Unwanted Lessons

Sometimes, we unexpectedly fall in love, and
sometimes people unexpectedly fall out of it.
Like a missed flight,
sometimes, we are left staring at the sky,
standing alone while the other person moved on; yet
all things still seem to come together for the best, and
that, I am certain.

Unspoken Words

I once lost someone unexpectedly. The person was gone, so my last words to them were never said. I can still feel the words heavy on my chest. I can still remember thinking "Should I say it now or next time?" Come to find out, there was never a next time. Sometimes, your vulnerability is worth your peace of mind.

Tides of Tears

Sometimes, we go through battles that can't be seen, dealing with the tides of war similar to a movie scene, but we keep a straight face so the world can't see. So she keeps it all together. He keeps it all together. But on the inside, they are self-destructing—doing things out of character. She ignores the feeling and excuses it as a new chapter. He's upset because he's dealing with personal issues. Stop, step back, and breathe. Let it all out, and know it's always cloudy before the sun.

Grown-Up Puppy Love

We played under the covers like teenagers;
But I guess things change and feelings fade.
Now, our time is done,
like a beautiful sunset that soon goes pitch black.
I guess we no longer see eye to eye.
It's crazy how time flies.
The good goes with the bad,
but I wish you the best.

Truth, Love, Lies

I told her things to make her better.
I told her things she didn't want to hear.
It would have been a lot better if those things didn't
make her leave,
only to appreciate me long after the sunset.

Already Gone

If someone comes to you unprovoked and tells you they want to leave, let them go. They have already settled at their new location.

The Truth Still Hurts

After a breakup, no explanation is an explanation.
Take it and run.

Running

She started off way too comfortable.
The last time she felt that way, it didn't end well.
So she had to go.
She had to leave before another heartache.

Patience

Butterflies, caring, emotions—
feeling those things can feel good.
But after a breakup, you cannot rush those feelings
with someone new.
You cannot rush what's organic.
Your heart will soon call your bluff.

Chapter Three: Healing/Inspiration

The Butterfly Effect

A butterfly flew by me today.
It made me think about time.
The time when I wasn't where I am today.
The time when I dreamed of doing what I did today.
And I thought,
"How quickly does the life of a butterfly go by.
It spends all this time trying to become what it was
meant to be,
only to relish in its moment for a short period of time."

And then I thought,
"Have I reached my full potential yet?"
And the obvious answer was
"No. I'm still striving to be a better me."
So, like a butterfly, there must be moments
where the caterpillar rejoices and appreciates the gains
it made.
And then I thought,
"How different are we from a butterfly?"

Things Found after the Fire

Some people say fire destroys, but to me, it rebuilds. Because when I lost everything, I found the mentality to persevere and the strength to not give up. I discovered skills that I didn't know existed in me. I was like an old piece of wood reclaimed, born to start new again.

Orphan

His mind is frozen on the page as he reads line by line. His fingertips touch the book page by page as time drips on by. The lady in the background hollers, "Go outside and play." But his mind takes him on a trip way past the front steps of the orphanage on McCarter Drive.

Whenever I Fall

I have fallen seven times and have gotten up ten. Even when I thought I was up, Jesus still lifted me up higher.

Understanding of Time

Time is like water in the palm of your hand.
The tighter you try to grab it, the faster it goes.
If you understand the water in the palm of your hand,
you will surely understand time.
It doesn't matter how you hold the water,
it will surely evaporate.
Hold the water in such a way that it can be managed.

Your Destiny

Don't worry; the very same reasons you're upset right now are going to be the very same reasons you make it. Sometimes, uncomfortable situations accelerate change.

You'll Get It Back

The world is often like your body. What you put into it is often what you get back.

Don't Pretend

Pain, when it's not taken care of, can become a flood.
You close one door pretending the pain is gone,
but it leaks into the next room
Before you know it, you're standing in the flood.
Don't carry your baggage into your present after the
lesson is learned.

Falling Rain

There is calmness in the sound of falling rain. The sound soothes my mind and fills me with serenity.

This Season

Without happiness, would there be sorrow?
Or without the experience of sorrow, would you know happiness?
In life, we all have different seasons.
Learn from your seasons, and rejoice in the harvest.

Blink

Those who know me understand that I seldom boast or brag, if at all. I learned at a young age that anything can be taken away in the blink of an eye. My understanding of things will always be my teacher. To God be the glory.

Walking in the Sky

No roads were paved, and no yellow lines were drawn. But ever since I had that dream, I did everything I could to make that dream a reality, and that has made all the difference.

The Beauty of Solitude

Take time to think; take time to understand what you really want. Take time to understand that there is gold within your veins; take time to understand you have power over your negative thoughts.

Mind-set

Sometimes, poverty can be a state of mind that all the money and gold can't cure. First, you must release your mind to understand wealth.

Dreams

Dreams become reality; reality turns into more dreams.

Slow Down

When life is on cruise control and then hits a speed bump, we often get upset. However, without that speed bump, we could have cruised past our destination.

His Last Words

Your lips have many words, but your breath can only murmur a few. You chose wisely. Like the morning sunlight slowly drifting away, your body can no longer enjoy the taste of life. You're faced with the expectation of expecting the utterly unexpected when you close your eyes for the last time. And as you begin to murmur your last words, serenity abounds, and you feel it. Ultimately, we all go; let people know you care when you can.

Thinking

Sometimes, a person and his or her thoughts are worth its weight in gold.

How to Get Over a Breakup

Step one: Let go of that person.
Have no expectations from that person.
No expectations, means no disappointments.

Step two: Give it time.
It takes time to heal; give it time.
I promise you'll be fine.

Step three: Heal.
Pick up a new skill, get in shape, and so on.
Work on things you're passionate about.
Remember, your self-worth is not determined by
someone else's opinion.

What Have You Missed?

Like a passing train, we are always on the go.
Although we may see the scenery, we never really
experience the scenery. Today, take the time and look
at the things around you. You may be surprised by
what you've been missing.

Let the Past Bury the Past

Sometimes, it's best not to reflect on past situations or memories. Those belong to yesterday; focus on the present, and create new memories. Yesterday is already gone. If you look ahead, you can enjoy the view much better.

You Can Fly

I know he hurt you.
But just like the sun that comes up in the morning,
you will rise again.
You will heal again.
You can get over another heartbreak.
This pain does not define you.
You're beautiful.

Stamina

Stamina. Such a simple word that bears so much meaning. It's a requirement for success, and the lack of it oftentimes leads to failure. So I have learned to keep my eyes on the prize and just keep going. I'm stubborn that way.

Brushstrokes

Sometimes the strokes of a picture can be painted
effortlessly, carefully, and almost perfectly.
However, the beauty of the picture still cannot be seen.
Just like diligently working and not seeing the results.
Not because it was not painted correctly or because
you did something wrong—
it simply needed enough time to dry.

Sometimes, you have to just keep painting.
Know that in time, each color will set.
Then the beauty of your work will be seen.
Sometimes the only difference between
disappointment and success
is timing.
Continue painting, and allow the process to settle.

Gentle Words

Sometimes, the biggest impact on someone's day can be the simplest of words.

Appreciation

Sometimes, it takes a little bit of sorrow to appreciate the happiness that's coming down the road.

Her Strength and His Shame

She lay there as if frozen in time, consumed by her emotions.
She felt a guilt that wasn't hers to bear.
It was his shame and his alone.
She decided moments later that
it was her strength that was going to define her and nothing else.
There's something special about a woman's perseverance.

You Actually Walked Away

The fact that they walked away was all the motivation you needed to not give up.

Soar

Be free.
Fly.
Use your own judgment.
Use wisdom.
Live and leave the world in your whirlwind.
You were made to let your colors shine.
So just breathe and be free.
Free to fly.

One-Way Ticket

She took a trip
with a one-way ticket in hand,
with no plan,
with only a feeling that everything would be all right.
She had dreams money couldn't buy.

Oprah

She was told she didn't have the right look—
that she wasn't the right fit.
Instead of accepting their reality,
she accepted hers and took a leap of faith.
Today, people call her Oprah.
She believed, and maybe you can too.

If You Only Tried

Imagine being free to actually try that thing you've
been dreaming about.
Imagine taking that leap of faith.
Imagine leaving all your fears behind.
Imagine.

Success Can Hurt

Don't be afraid to fail.
Don't be afraid to fall.
Could birds fly if they are scared of heights?
Be afraid only when failing becomes an expectation.

Home Cooking for the Soul

Guard your dreams;
protect your heart.
Those things nourish your soul.

One of Those Days

Sometimes, I don't have the energy to put up a fight.
Sometimes, I prefer to stay in some nights.
Sometimes, I just keep thinking everything will be all
right.
Sometimes, I just play dumb so I don't have to
entertain a fool
because I can, quietly, be right.

There's a Difference

Everyone has an answer, but not too many people have a solution.

Facts versus Reality

Please keep this in mind: every negative thought that echoes through your mind doesn't have to be right.

That Really Hurt

Sometimes, inspiration comes from being hurt.
The healing comes from following through on that inspiration.
Sometimes, motivation comes from hurt that we endure.

Lost and Found

You lost that person, but you had to in order to find that new person who takes your breath away, in ways you never imagined.

Let's See

The hardest part is letting go
after putting in so much work,
like an engine that no longer works.
The hardest part is getting out the car and facing the
reality.
It's okay to let go of a relationship that no longer
works
even after you put in all that work. Despite the hurt,
it's okay to let it go.

Faith

You are like a plant that starts to grow between
concrete bricks.
Because even if they try to build barriers around you,
nothing will stop you.
Nothing can prevent you from reaching your
purpose—
not even concrete bricks.

Stuff Happens

Shit happens. Don't sweat it—nothing can prevent you from reaching your purpose; the only one who can stop you is you.

The Right Time

Timing.
Everything you are going through now is preparing you for the right timing.
The right timing for new opportunities, new relationships.
Don't sweat the small stuff.
Old situations need to finish for new ones to start.

Love Does

Be quiet.
Listen, not to words.
But look at their actions.
Their actions are always truer than their words.

Gold

Some like the glitter;
Some like the gold.
Remember
it takes substance to stand tall.

A New Special Someone

After a breakup, the best person to meet is not someone else.
The best person to meet is your new self.

Consistency

Remember that time you wanted that thing to happen and it didn't? You later realized why it didn't happen, and you were happy. Well yeah, that's life. Sometimes you may not realize that current *disappointment* is really a *blessing* in disguise. Keep dreaming, keep working, and give it time. Consistency is key.

Golden Girl

So it was then she realized that all these heartaches
and tribulations were preparing her for the biggest
opportunity of her life. Sometimes, the fire acts as fuel
to take you to a higher purpose.

I Know Love

When you know your worth, you accept a lot less discounts from people who don't deserve you.

Old Things New

I took a trip to Cuba, and I found beauty in things old.
Modernized people living in decayed buildings. Some
are unplugged from the world, yet their minds seemed
to be moving with the times. I wondered,
Is it really us who have been standing still? In Cuba,
their world appeared a little less filtered. I saw people
in their rawest form: the good, the bad, the indifferent,
and the beautiful.

Ignore Them

You can live a much happier life when you ignore the negative comments made by others. Some people, due to their insecurities, transfer their negativity to you with comments meant to get under your skin. Sometimes, stupidity needs no response.

Muscle Pain

Growth takes change, and change can hurt.

Let It Go

Time can heal both physical and emotional pain.
But most importantly, don't keep reopening old
wounds.
Focus on the positive.
Let go of all that hurt.
You're worth more.

Time

Time is the ultimate currency. Don't spend it over analyzing about people who have already moved on.

Patiently Living

There is an art to being
patient.
Good things sometimes take
time.

No Comment

Not all stupid comments deserve a response. Sometimes, not being bothered by ignorance is worth it.

Push

Many things start as a dream, then an action taken, then a setback, then a break through, and then success. You don't have to stop at any of the steps before success.

Counted in Twice

When I was eight, a bee stung me on my right eye.
I walked around with a swollen right eye for an entire
week.
That's exactly how I felt when you left—
stunned and uncomfortable.
But just like my eye,
I knew my heart would heal.
But the thing is the motivation to succeed without you
has never left me.
You counted me out,
so I counted myself in twice. And for that, I am
forever grateful.

Appointed Time

Everything has an appointed time.
Forget the forecast; forget your expectation of time.
Understand every tear you shed is accounted for; every
pain you endured has its place. Trust your purpose,
and know your time will soon be upon you.
Just know sometimes good things come when you
least expect it, but understand it's on its way.

Today

Today is a good day to be happy. Today is a good day
for a great day.

Dear Reader, we have reached the end of this journey, but this is just the beginning.

For excerpts and updates, please follow
Instagram.com/Thepoetryzone.